For Dyana and Ricky,

in loving memory of Valentina

1

The Author: Photo V. Pokorny

THE COMMONPLACE BOOK
OF A LANCASHIRE LAD

GLEANINGS FROM A LIFE OF
LOOKING AND LISTENING

by

DOUGLAS PILLING

AuthorHouse™ UK Ltd.
500 Avebury Boulevard
Central Milton Keynes, MK9 2BE
www.authorhouse.co.uk
Phone: 08001974150

First published by AuthorHouse 05/03/2010

ISBN: 978-1-4490-7068-7 (sc)

This book is printed on acid-free paper.

For many years I have kept a note-book in which I have written things that have caught my fancy either because I enjoyed them, but mostly because I agreed with them. I have now decided it is time to share them; they gave me much pleasure and guidance and hopefully they will do the same for you.

I am a product of a Lancashire working-class upbringing, my childhood was spent in Fish and Chip shops which my parents had, first in Oswaldtwistle and then in Burnley. We moved around; a village school led to Grammar School, which led to University, and then joining a Lancashire cotton manufacturing company, "going through the mill" as a management trainee; then a year in the U.S. which led to meeting and marrying a girl from Guatemala and working and living in Latin America.

There I continued my life-long interest in hill-walking and mountain climbing and also became interested and involved in pre-Columbian archeology, particularly in the Maya which had left many magnificent ruins and artefacts in Guatemala and a talented Indian population.
But at heart I am still a Lancashire lad and still have a house in the village where I spent my youth and where I still feel at home.

TRANEARTH

A. R. JOHNSON

One mustn't lose sight of the hard core, which is, do this, do that, love your friends and like your neighbours, be just, be extravagantly generous, be honest, be tolerant, have courage, have compassion, use your wits and your imagination, understand the world you live in and be on terms with it, don't dramatize and dream of escape.

After all, life, for all its agonies of despair and loss and guilt, is exciting and beautiful, amusing and artful and endearing, full of liking and of love, at times a poem and a high adventure, at times noble and at times very gay; and whatever (if anything) is to come after it, we shall not have this life again.

Rose Macaulay "The Towers of Trebizond"

Honister and Fleetwith Pike from Grey Crag - Birkness Coombe

Ars long, vita brevis . . . ." full translation:-
"Life is short, life is long, you must act at the
right moment, experiment is dangerous and
judgement difficult"
(This text apparently comes from ancient
Greek doctors who were remarkable for
being prepared to describe their failures as
well as their successes)

Hippocrates
(c460-357BC)

A little coitus never hoitus

Dorothy Parker

Women are like horses – best when they've summat to do.

Farmer, owner of a good restaurant in Edenfield, Lancashire. He has five daughters, all working for him in the business

Human speech is at bottom no more than the individual's demand for reassurance in a lonely world; the sophisticated contrive to extract comforting intimations of solidarity from disagreement, controversy and repartee; the uninstructed prefer much simpler forms of mutual support. When the ritual is in course of celebration it is a solecism to break the grand affirmative flow of things, and indeed we none of us particularly care for the man who qualifies our suggestion that it is a fine day, or that it looks like rain, or that it is nice to see a little bit of sunshine.
"The Daffodil Affair" Michael Innes

Use your health, even to the point of wearing yourself out. That is what it is for. Spend all you have before you die; do not outlive yourself.

George Bernard Shaw

One thing I've learned as I get older is just go ahead and do it. It is much easier to apologize after something's been done than to get permission ahead of time.

Grace Murray Hopper (Rear Admiral)

We don't stop playing because we grow old; we grow old because we stop playing.

George Bernard Shaw

Don't ever save anything for a special occasion. Being alive is a special occasion.

Avril Sloe

A.E.JOHNSON

LAKE DISTRICT

12

"*Navigare necesse est vivere non necesse*"

Isak Dinesen's motto, which was Pompey's address to his crew. (It is necessary to sail; it is not necessary to live)

It's better to keep your mouth shut and appear stupid than open your mouth and disperse all doubts.

Mark Twain

La sabiduriao nos llega cuando ya no nos sirve de nada.

Wisdom comes to us when it is no longer any use.

Gabriel Garcia Marquez

Moderation in all things, including moderation.

Shy bairns get nowt.
(A Newcastle version of 'Faint heart never won fair lady')

Lliwedd from Llyn Glaslyn, Snowdonia

Simplicity is the ultimate sophistication.

Leonardo da Vinci

*To know someone here or there with whom
you can feel there is understanding in spite
of distances or thoughts unexpressed – that
can make of this earth a garden.*

Goethe

*You cannot stay on the summit forever. You
have to come down again . . . one climbs
and one sees; one descends and one sees no
longer, but one has seen. There is an art in
conducting oneself . . . by the memory of
what one saw higher up, when one no
longer sees, one can at least still know.*

René Daumal

Aspire not to have more but to be more.
Archbisop Romero
(via Julian Filochowski)

A nation has a history, a culture, an identity. Britain is not France, Spain is not Germany, and none of these are Bangladesh or Morocco. Nor do their citizens want them to become so. People do not want to be overrun by foreigners of a strange religion, a different race, or exotic (and sometimes repulsive) customs, even if it means a 1% rise in economic growth, no amount of lecturing will change these attitudes.

A letter to "The Economist" January 2008

Not everything that counts can be counted and not everything that can be counted counts.

A sign posted on the door of Einstein's office

Nobody ever got to the end of their life and said "I wish I'd spent more time at work".

Meg Monn (British Foreign Office)

There is a fountain of youth: it is your mind, your talents, the creativity you bring to your life and to the people you love.

Sophia Loren

*O God, our help in ages past, our hope for
years to come,
Our shelter from the stormy blast, and our
eternal home.
Beneath the shadow of Thy throne, Thy
saints have dwelt secure;
Sufficient is Thine arm alone, and our
defence is sure.
Time, like and ever-rolling stream, bears all
its sons away,
They fly forgotten as a dream dies at the
opening day.
A thousand ages in Thy sight are like an
evening gone;
Short as the watch that ends the night,
before the rising sun.
O God our help in ages past, our hope for
years to come,
Be Thou our guide while life shall last, and
our eternal home. Amen.*

*Isaac Watts
(Sung as a choir boy)*

*I wish we were not so single-minded about
keeping our lives moving, and for once
could do nothing, perhaps a huge silence
might interrupt this sadness of never
understanding ourselves and of threatening
ourselves with death.*

*Pablo Neruda
(Probably better in Spanish)*

The Flying Dutchman
Poldubh Crags-Glen Nevis

Chaos often breeds life, where order breeds habit.

Henry Adams

It's never too late to do nothing

Zen saying

Death destroys man, but the idea of death saves him.

E. M. Forster

A sense of the comic is the most valuable contribution that the English have to offer anywhere

Nichola Freeling
"No part in your Death"

It ain't what people don't know that hurts them, it's what they do know that ain't so.

Mark Twain

*He was obviously endowed with that
wonderful quality which is called KAYF –
the contemplation which comes of silence
and ease. It is not meditation or reverie,
which presupposes a conscious mind
relaxing; it is something deeper a
fathomless repose of the will which does not
even pose to itself the question: 'Am I happy
or unhappy?'*

"Bitter Lemons" ; Lawrence Durrell

*No es la riqueza
Ni el esplendor
Sino la tranquilidad
Y el deber cumplido
Los que nos brindan
La felicidad**

*Hung on the wall of the tailor
"Principe de Gales" Guatemala*

*   *It is not riches
Nor splendour
But tranquillity
And one's duty done
That brings us
Happiness.*

Old age is not for sissies.

(Bette Davis)

Defecatio matutina bona tamquam serotina
Defecatio serotina bona tamquam matutina
Defecatio meridiana neque bona neque
sana.

Ovid
From Scipio Merler (Trekking round
Annapurna)

Teach us delight in simple things
And mirth that has no bitter springs.

Rudyard Kipling

It is not enough to despise the world. Not
enough to live life as though riches and
power were nothings. They are not. But to
grasp, feel the world grow great in the
grasp is not enough either. The secret is to
grasp and then let go.

Chinese and antique from
"The Seacoast of Bohemia";
Nicholas Freeling

Trinity Slabs · Wallowbarrow

Jim Rostron Climbing

Home is where the food comes on the table.

Turkish saying, Nicholas Freeling

Dying is matter of slapstick and prat falls.
The ageing process is not gradual or gentle.
It rushes up, pushes you over and runs off
laughing. No one should grow old who isn't
ready to appear ridiculous.

John Mortimer
"The Summer of a Dormouse"

La vida es un trancazo
Que al fin y al cabo nos doma
Porqué no salir del paso
Y tomarlo como una broma?*

Alfonso Morales
Tourist entrepreneur, Palenque, Mexico

*   *Life is a risky slide*
       Which at the end we get broke
       Why not step on one side
       And take it as a joke?

B R JOHNSON

KILNSEY CRAG

Prose is the achievement of civilization, or people who have learned to discuss without blows or invective, who know that truth is hard to find and worth finding, who do not begin by accusing an opponent of wickedness, but elicit reason and patience by displaying them. Civilization may not surpass a primitive society in heights of rapture or heroism, but it is, if it be civilization, better for everyday life, kinder, more rational, more sustained in effort.

Arthur Clutton-Brock
"The defects of English Prose"

Without measureless and perpetual uncertainty the drama of human life would be destroyed.

Winston Churchill

Courage is rightly esteemed the first of human qualities because it is the quality which guarantees all others.

Winston Churchill

There is only one real luxury, that of human relationships.

> *Saint Exupéry*

Harold: You certainly have a way with people!
Maude: Well – they're my species.

> *The film "Harold and Maude"*

They say the seeds of what we will do are in all of us, but it always seems to me that in those who make jokes in life the seeds are covered with better soil and with a higher grade of manure.

> *Ernest Hemmingway*
> *"A Moveable Feast"*

Doing business without advertising is like winking at a girl in the dark. You know what you are going, but nobody else does.

> *Stewart Henderson Britt*

Men are made stronger on realization that the helping hand they need is at the end of their own right arm.

Sydney J. Phillips

*The moving finger writes; and having writ,
Moves on; nor all thy piety nor wit
Shall lure it back to cancel half a line,
Nor all thy tears wash out a word of it.*

Edward Fitzgerald

It is a mistake to look too far ahead. Only one link in the chain of destiny can be handled at a time.
Winston Churchill

It is no use saying "We are doing our best". You have to succeed in doing what is necessary.

Winston Churchill

A. R. JOHNSON

The Grandes Jorasses from Aiguille de Grépon

28

*Cricket is a game that the English, not being
a spiritual people, have invented to give
themselves a conception of eternity.*
                                    Lord Mancroft

*It is part of English hypocrisy – or English
reserve – that, while we are fluent enough
in grumbling about small inconveniences,
we insist in making light of any great
difficulties or griefs that beset us.*
                                    Max Beerbohm

*One of those untrammelled Victorian
adventurers, usually high born but
inexplicably inured to discomfort, whose
curiosity moves them to treat continents as
obvious maps of the Old Boy network and
treks into deserts and remote mountain
valleys as suburban excursions.*

*"The Last Lion", William Manchester
(A biography of Churchill, but applicable to
Ian Graham)*

CIR - MHOR   2618 ft.   ARRAN

A.K.JOHNSON

Democracy is the best system of government yet devised but it suffers from one grave defect. It does not encourage those military values on which, in an envious world, it must frequently depend for survival

A French Officer

God must have loved the common man, he made so many of them, but it is uncommon men and women who, when nations get in danger, as they invariably do, must come to the fore and lead.

Abraham Lincoln

The knowledge of death gives intensity to middle age as passion and hope gives intensity to youth.

I don't believe any relationship can succeed that doesn't offer both partners solitude and independence as a matter of course.

"Sweet Death, Kind Death", Amanda Cross

BOON BECK

A.R. JOHNSON

Speech is Silver, Silence is Golden.

Swiss inscription

We sleep safe in our beds because rough men stand ready in the night to visit violence on those who would do us harm.

George Orwell

I was to learn later in life that we tend to meet any new situation by reorganizing; and a wonderful method it can be for creating the illusion of progress while producing confusion, inefficiency and demoralization.

Petronius Arbiter

The most unhappy of all men is the man who has got no work cut-out for him in the world, and does not go into it. For work is the grand cure of all the maladies and miseries that ever beset mankind – honest work, which you intend getting done.
Thomas Carlyle

SCAFELL PINNACLE

A.R. JOHNSON

Work – the great flywheel of Society.

Sigmund Freud

*There are three kinds of lies: lies, damned
lies and statistics.*

*Attributed to Disraeli
in Mark Twain's "Autobiography"*

*One of the greatest disservices you can do to
a man is to lend him money that he can't
pay back.*

Jesse H. James

*Earl of Sandwich: " ' pon my honour,
Wilkes, I don't know whether you will die
upon the gallows or of the pox"
John Wilkes: "That depends my Lord,
whether I first embrace your Lordship's
principles, or your Lordship's mistresses"*

*If you compare yourself with others, you
may become vain or bitter, for always there
will be greater or lesser persons than
yourself.*

Desiderata (Ehrmann)

*There are three things which are real: God,
human folly and laughter. Since the first
two pass our comprehension, we must do
what we can with the third.*

The Ramayana

*For myself I am an optimist – it doesn't
seem much use being anything else.*

Winston Churchill

*It is said that an Eastern monarch once
charged his wise men to invent him a
sentence to be ever in view, which should be
true and appropriate in all times and
situations. They presented him with the
words; "And this, too, shall pass away".
How much it expresses! How chastening in
the hour of pride! – how consoling in the
depth of affliction!*

Abraham Lincoln and older sources

*The fundamental question for the United
States is how it can co-operate to help meet
the basic needs of the people of the
hemisphere despite the philosophical
disagreements it may have with the nature
of particular regimes. It must seek
pragmatic ways to help people without
necessarily embracing their governments. It
should recognise that diplomatic relations
are merely practised conveniences and not a
measure of moral judgement.*

Nelson A. Rockefeller

*Many forms of government have been tried,
and will be tried in this world of sin and
woe. No one pretends that democracy is
perfect or all-wise. Indeed it has been said
that democracy is the worst form of
government except all those other forms
that have been tried from time to time.*

Winston Churchill

*I slept
And dreamt that life was all joy
I awoke
And saw that life was but service
I served
And understood that service was joy.*

Tagore

Art, to exist in any form, must give pleasure.

W. H. Auden

A basic rule of American conversation - one may be serious or frivolous, but never both in the same paragraph.

Nicholas Blake

Old age isn't so bad when you consider the alternative.

Maurice Chevalier

For forms of government let fools contest;
Whate'er is best administered is best
For modes of faith let graceless zealots fight
This can't be wrong whose life is in the right
In faith and hope the world will disagree,
But all mankind's concern is charity.

Pope

There lives more faith in honest doubt,
Believe me, than in half the creeds.

Tennyson

When I was a child I spoke as a child, I
understood as a child, I thought as a child;
but when I became a man I put away
childish things.
For now we see through a glass darkly; but
then face to face: now I know in part but
then shall I know even also as I am known.
And now abideth faith, hope and charity,
these three; but the greatest of these is
charity. [x]

1ˢᵗ Epistle, Paul to the Corinthians

• *The modern translation of the word "charity " is "love"*

In a perfect union the man and woman are
like a string bow. Who is to say whether the
string bends the bow, or the bow tightens
the string?

Complacent mental laziness is the English
disease.

The Etive Beinn Trilleachan Slabs

A. R. Johnson

The secret of happiness lies in the avoidance of Angst (anxiety, spleen, guilt, fear, remorse). It is a mistake to consider happiness as a positive state. By removing Angst, the condition of all unhappiness, we are then prepared to receive any blessings to which we are entitled.

Les pretentions sont une source de peiner, et l'epoque du bonheur de la vie commence au moment on ellles finisent.

Nicolas Chamfort

Life is a tragedy to those who feel, but a comedy to those who think.

Horace Walpole

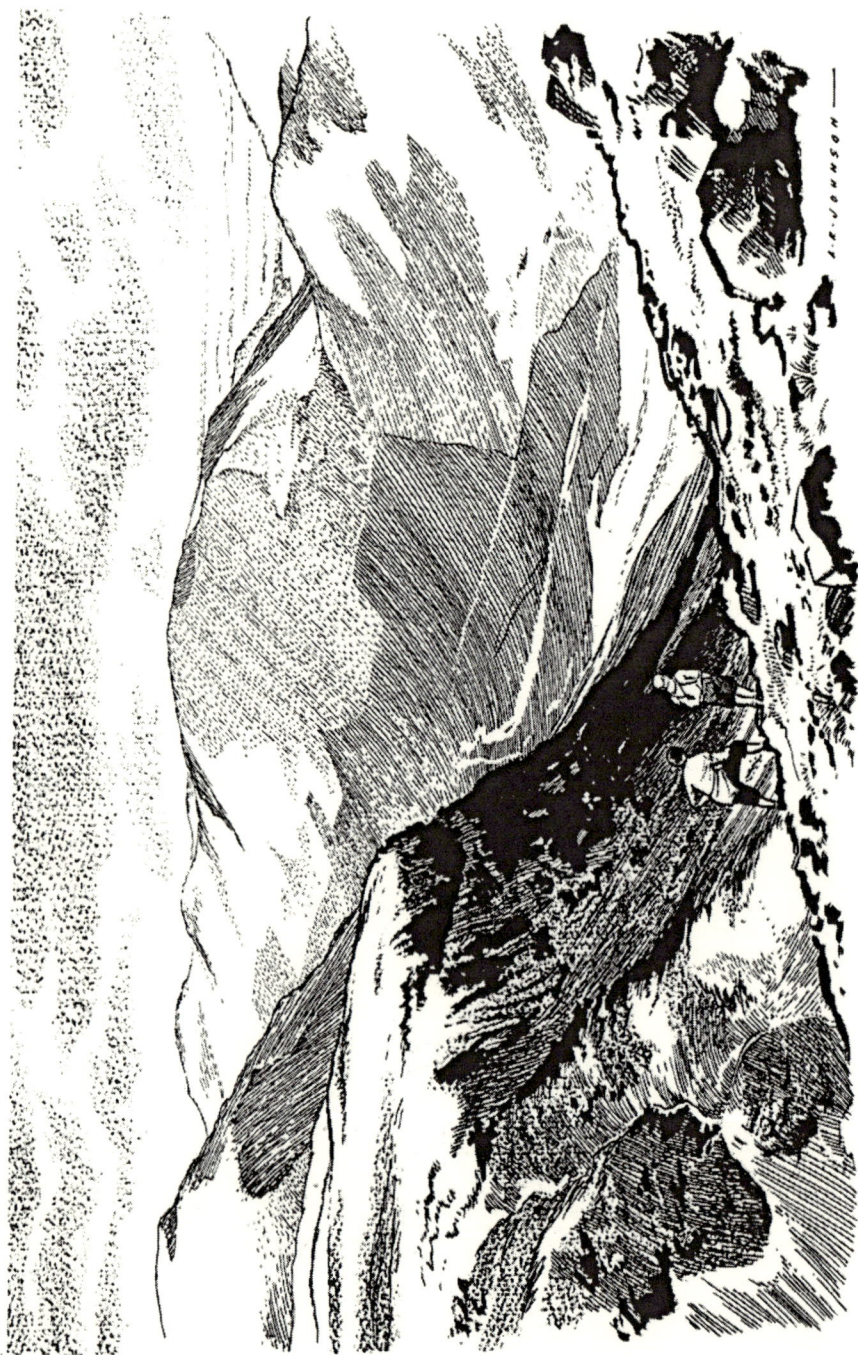

LOOKING DOWN ENNERDALE FROM GREAT GABLE

R. LEVENSON

42

Excerpts from "The Unquiet Grave" (Cyril Connolly)

Those of us who were brought up as Christians and who have lost our faith have retained the Christian sense of sin without the saving belief of redemption.

The secret of happiness (and therefore success) is to be in harmony with existence, to be always calm, always lucid, always willing.

The friendships that last are those wherein each friend respects the other's dignity to the point of not really wanting anything from him. Therefore a man with a will to power can have no friends. He is like a boy with a chopper. He tries it on flowers, he tries it on sticks, he tries is on furniture and at last he breaks it on stone.

It is easy . . . . terribly easy . . . . to shake a man's faith in himself. To take advantage of that, to break a man's spirit, is devil's work.

George Bernard Shaw

Live all you can; it's a mistake not to. It doesn't so much matter what you do in particular, so long as you have your life. If you haven't had that, what have you had?
Henry James
(not very well put – Rose Macaulay said it better)

The art of being wise is knowing what to overlook.
William James

If you don't get everything you want, think of the things you don't get that you don't want.

Oscar Wilde

Good people are good because they have come to wisdom through failure. We get very little wisdom from success, you know.

William Saroyan

When I was a young man I observed that nine out of ten things I did were failures. I didn't want to be a failure, so I did ten times more work.

George Bernard Shaw

The manner in which one endures what must be endured is more important than the thing that must be endured.

Dean Acheson

Blessed are those that heal us of self-despairing. Of all the services that can be done to man, I know of none more precious.

William Hale White

DOW CRAG from Cove Bridge, Torver Beck

46

*There's nothing worth the wear of winning
but laughter and the love of friends.*

Hilaire Belloc

*There is nothing noble about being superior
to some other man. True nobility is being
superior to your precious self.*

Samuel Johnson

*The English are insular, not so much in the
sense of being insolent but simply of being
ignorant; but they are not spiteful.*
G. K. Chesterton

The Selkirk Grace

*"Some hae meat an' canna eat,
And some wad eat that want it,
But we hae meat an' can eat
Sae let the Lord be thankit"*

Robert Burns

Lake District

48

The one important thing I have learned over the years is the difference between taking one's work seriously and taking one's self seriously. The first is imperative and the second is disastrous.

> *Margot Fonteyn*

When we are not sure, we are alive.

> *Graham Greene*

Said by the diner swindled in a restaurant:

So I leave you, poorer sadder,
Lest you make me poorer still;
Sharper than the biting adder
Is the adder of the bill.
> *Adrian Ross*

Supreme egotism and utter seriousness are necessary for the greatest accomplishment, and these the Irish find hard to sustain; at some point, the instinct to see life in a comic light becomes irresistible, and ambition falls before it.

> *William V. Shannon*

Truth can understand error; but error cannot understand truth.

Lord Hugh Cecil

Many of the Spanish, like many of the English, had been rulers of whom any Empire might be proud.

Cunninghame Graham

Boiled cabbage a l'Anglaise is something compared with which steamed coarse newsprint bought from bankrupt Finnish salvage dealers and heated over smokey oil stoves is an exquisite delicacy. Boiled British cabbage is something lower than ex-Army blankets stolen by dispossessed Goanese doss-house keepers who used them to cover busted-down hen houses in the slum district of Karachi, found them useless and threw them in anger into the Indes, where they were recovered by convicted beachcombers with grappling irons, who cut them into strips with shears and stewed them in sheep dip before they were sold to dying beggars. Boiled cabbage!

Cassandra (William Connor)

*In 1765 M. Boulanger sold good soup in his
Dining Room in Paris and put up a board
"Venite ad me; vos que stomacho laboratis
et ego restaurato vos" (Come to me with
laboured stomachs and I will restore you)
The soup became known as a restaurant
(restorative); the word came to be applied
to the Dining Room and finally to any
Dining Room supplying good food.*

　　　　　　　　　Robert Smith Surtees

*The modern painting has been made by
writers: if they would only keep quiet it
would disappear.*

　　　　　　　　　　　　Paul Valéry

*Klee's pictures seem to me to resemble, not
pictures, but a sample book of patterns of
linoleum.*

　　　　　　　　　　　Cyril Asquith

*Abstract art? A product of the untalented,
sold by the unprincipled to the utterly
bewildered.*

　　　　　　　　　　　　　Al Capp

Red Tarn and Helvellyn

A. R. JOHNSON

52

Because they have no sun, the English can
be neither philosophers nor artists: they
have no spark of constructive (synthetic)
genius.

Oliveira Martins

"White wine" he used to say dogmatically "is
bad, it cuts the legs".

Edward Whymper, quoting his guide

Art is art, and nothing can be done to
prevent it. But there is the Mayoress's
decency to be considered.

The Mayor of a Lancashire town,
on being presented with a pair of
nude statues for his Town Hall

DERWENTWATER AND SKIDDAW FROM ASHNESS BRIDGE

A classic – something that everybody wants to have read and nobody wants to read.

Mark Twain

Those who have free seats at the play hiss first.

Chinese Proverb

All the arts in America are a gigantic racket run by unscrupulous men for unhealthy women.

Thomas Beecham

There are moments when art attains almost to the dignity of manual labour.

Oscar Wilde

True education makes for inequality; the inequality of individuality, the inequality of success; the glorious inequality of talent, of genius; for inequality, not mediocrity, individual superiority, not standardization, is the measure of the progress of the world.

Felix E. Schelling

Many have said that Homer never existed and others have replied that his works were written by another Greek poet of the same name.

Frank Muir

Biography, like big game hunting, is one of the recognised forms of sport, and it is unfair as only sport can be.

Philip Guedalla

*Disraeli's standard reply when sent an
unsolicited manuscript: "Many thanks; I
shall lose no time in reading it".*

*It is good to be on your guard against an
Englishman who speaks French perfectly;
he is very likely to be a card-sharper or an
attaché in the diplomatic service.*

W. Somerset Maugham

TRANEARTH - TORVER

58

*A critic is a man who knows the way but
can't drive the car.*

Kenneth Tynan

A critic: A louse in the locks of literature.

Tennyson

*Parsifal – The kind of opera that starts at 6
o'clock and after it has been going three
hours, you look at your watch and it says
6.20.*

David Randolph

*Education – that which discloses to the wise
and disguises from the foolish their lack of
understanding.*

Ambrose Bierce

*The Battle of Yorktown was lost on the
playing fields of Eton.*

H. Allen Smith

*Education is the process of casting false
pearls before real swine.*

Irwin Edman

*Backward travels our gaze .... back
through the brash adventurous days of the
first Elizabeth and the hard materialism of
the Tudors, and then at last we find them ...
in many a village church, beneath ... the
coffered ceiling of the chantry chapel. From
brass and stone, from line and effigy; their
eyes look out at us, and as we gaze into
them, as we would win some answer from
their inscrutable silence. "Tell us what it is
that binds us together; show us the clue that
leads through a thousand years; whisper to
us the secret of this charmed life of England,
that we in our time may know how to hold it
fast."*

Enoch Powell

Music – it is the only sensual pleasure
without vice.

Boswell

She was a town and country soprano of the
kind often used for augmenting grief at a
funeral.

George Ade

"All we have is one another and if we are
orphans all we can honourably do is adopt
one another, defy the meaninglessness of
our lives by mutual concern. It is the only
nobility we have."

William McIlvanney "The Papers of Tony
Veitch"

"The law, morality and common-sense meet
at few crossroads."

Frances Fyfield "A Question of Guilt"

"Hearts that are delicate and kind and
tongues that are neither – these make the
best company in the world."

L. Pearsall Smith

With or without religion, good people can behave well and bad people can do evil: but for good people to do evil – that takes religion.

Steven Weinberg

Penetrating so many secrets, we cease to believe in the unknowable. But there it sits nevertheless, calmly licking its chops.

H. L. Mencken

And thou wilt give thyself relief, if thou doest every act of thy life as if it were the last.

Marcus Aurelius

In the last analysis, it is our conception of death which decides our answers to all the questions that life puts to us.

Dag Hammarskjold

Life is painful, suffering is optional.

Sylvia Boorstein

HONISTER PASS CUMBRIA 1176 ft.
The Buttermere-side

A. R. JOHNSON—

Serendipity

"Searching for a needle in a haystack and instead finding the farmer's daughter."

*Que gran cosa es no hacer nada, y despues .
. . . . decansar* *

> *Old Spanish saying*
> *(Still currently in use)*

**What a great thing it is to do nothing, and afterward . . . . . rest*

ACKNOWLEDGEMENTS

My thanks are warmly given to Chris Aspin for his invaluable help to get this book printed and to Alan R. Johnson for providing the superb drawings which accompany the text. Many of the drawings were made relating to events of the Lancashire Caving and Climbing Club of which we are both members.

Further grateful thanks are due to Peter Jordan for his enduring friendship and never-failing help.

Lightning Source UK Ltd.
Milton Keynes UK
10 August 2010

158160UK00002B/54/P